D0719603

THIS IS A PARRAGON BOOK

© Parragon 1996
Reprinted in 1997

Parragon
13-17 Avonbridge Trading Estate
Atlantic Road, Avonmouth,
Bristol, BS11 9QD

Produced by The Templar Company plc,
Pippbrook Mill, London Road, Dorking
Surrey RH4 1JE

Designed by Mark Kingsley Monks

Printed and bound in Italy

ISBN 0 75252 066 0

THE
Jam Pandas'
FIRST BOOK OF
Weather

ILLUSTRATED BY STEPHANIE BOEY
WRITTEN BY CLAIRE STEEDEN

P

PARRAGON

Rain or shine,
the Jam Pandas have
fun whatever the
weather!

When it is **sunny**
Grandma eats
strawberry ice cream.

What is baby
Jim Jam eating?

When it is **cloudy**,
Pa looks for shapes
in the clouds.
What shapes can
you see?

Big Bamboo flies his kite when it is **windy**. What else is flying in the sky?

When it is **raining**, Jim Jam splashes in the puddles. What else is making a splash?

When it is **snowing**
Peaches and Plum
throw snowballs.
What have they made
with the snow?

Ma hides in bed when
there is **thunder** and
lightning.

Who else is hiding?

When it is **icy**, Aunt Apricot goes skating! Is she alone on the pond?

The Marmalade Cat
runs inside when there
are **hailstones**.
Who else is inside?

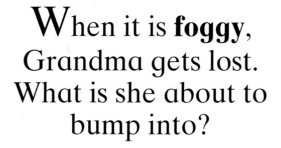

When it is **foggy**,
Grandma gets lost.
What is she about to
bump into?

When it rains at
the same time as the
sun shines, there
is a **rainbow**.

The Jam Pandas love
the beautiful colours.
Where does the
rainbow end?

Titles in this series include:

First Book of Animals

First Book of Colours

First Book of Counting

First Book of Opposites

First Book of Shapes

First Book of Weather